A World of Poetry

Table of Contents

Topsail by Holden Quinn	4	Fluffer by Harley Crumpler	38
Music by Madison Tart	5	Brothers by Harley Crumpler	39
Church by Marianne Moore	6	Replaced by Will Huff	40
Family by Brooke Raynor	7	Old Man Tan by Will Huff	40
Carolina by Gray Fussell	8	The Devil Himself by Will Huff	41
Frogs by Amos Lanier	9	A Change by Will Huff	42
Jesus by Harley Crumpler	10	The Snake and the Boy by Will Huff	43
Christian by Will Huff	11	Beach by Will Huff	43
Stealing Pete by Amos Lanier	12-13	The Spider by Will Huff	44
The Sun by Madison Tart	14-15	Bullet by Pelmon Hudson	44
Crash by Gray Fussell	16	Football by Pelmon Hudson	45
Earth by Will Huff	17	Sports by Gray Fussell	46
Sunrise, Sunset by Madison Tart	17	Beach by Gray Fussell	47
Landing by Billy Prestage	18	Muscadine by Gray Fussell	48
Home by Will Huff	18	Washey Will by Gray Fussell	49
Flowers by Marianne Moore	19	Swish by Gray Fussell	49
Shaking Legs by Harley Crumpler	19	Juicy Worm by Amos Lanier	50
Banana by Amos Lanier	20	Trains by Amos Lanier	50
Crazy by Pelmon Hudson	21	Deer by Amos Lanier	51
Book by Will Huff	21	My Love by Amos Lanier	52
Goodbye by Blake Daniel	22	Ray/Rhyming by Holden Quinn	53
Love by Madison Tart	22	Solo Flight by Holden Quinn	54 – 55
Caution by Madison Tart	23	Bear by Holden Quinn	56
Jesus by Brooke Raynor	24	Drip by Blake Daniel	57
Haikus	25 - 26	Field by Blake Daniel	58
My First Car Crash by Billy Prestage	27	Friends by Madison Tart	59
Winter by Brooke Raynor	27	Apology by Madison Tart	60
Bodie/Goose by Gray Fussell	28	Gorilla/Caterpillar by Madison Tart	61
Where I'm From Poems	29 - 35	Heartbreak by Madison Tart	62
The Balloon by Tyler Evans	36	Late by Marianne Moore	63
Summer Day by Tyler Evans	36	Grave by Marianne Moore	63
Animals by Tyler Evans	37	Septuplet by Marianne Moore	64
God by Harley Crumpler	37	Brothers by Brooke Raynor	65

America by Brooke Raynor	66
Whale by Brooke Raynor	67
Penny by Luke Burrows	68
Star by Luke Burrows	68
The Silky Moon by Joseph Lee	69
A Winter's Maiden by Joseph Lee	70
Songbird by Joseph Lee	71
Flower by Madison Guthrie	72
Chocolate by Anna Carson Quinn	73
Chocolate by Sam Hall	74
Sweet Temptations by Luke Burrows	75
Crunchy, Chewy, Chocolate by Anna Burgess	76
Spring by Hannah Buckner	77

Topsail

By Holden Quinn

The best place to be after May 24
Overall the best summer job
Plus the boat captain part is not bad
Sadly left on August 13
Although it is good to see people again
I will never forget the people from the sand
Left but not forgotten always to be remembered.

Music

By Madison Tart

Moves through your body
Uses words to
Say the things that are
Important
Causing your mind to think

Church

By Marianne Moore

Christians coming together
Helping others reach Christ
Understanding God's word
Reading the Bible
Carrying out the Great Commission
Honoring God with worship

Family

By Brooke Raynor

Forever they love me
Always they care for me
Magnificent people looking after me
I love them as well
Loving, you will always find
Yes they are mine forever

Carolina

By Gray Fussell

Carolina is
An awesome university that I
Really hope to attend
Oh, the thrill of
Living and learning
In Chapel Hill, I may
Never want to leave and I so hope my
Alma Mater will be U.N.C.!

Frogs

By Amos Lanier

Frogs are really pretty cool.
Ribbiting as they converse
On a log out in the swamp
Gobbling flies to fill their bellies
Sticky tongue to which the flies stick like glue

Jesus

By Harley Crumpler

Joyful Lord Almighty

Everlasting for all generations to learn

Savior of all Earth and

Universe. Look for Him and let Him in you

Sinners of all places, "He is coming! He is coming! Please prepare your hearts!"

Christian

By Will Huff

Cohering to the word of God
Helping others find their way
Raising others from the depths of sin
Involving thyself in church
Speaking Scripture to others
Testifying the truth
I will always love God
And no one can stop me
Never will I quit

Stealing Pete

By Amos Lanier

I once knew a man named Stealing Pete.
I never really liked that old cheat.
He stole everything because he was a thief.
He was hated very much by the local police chief.
He would steal things off the shelf in the store.
Put stuff in his pockets and walk right out the door.
He always got away with it because he was so sly.
Most people thought he was just a normal guy.
One day he tried to rob the general store,
But when he was walking out the door,
His stolen items fell to the floor.
The owner yelled, "You get back here!"
But Pete ran and dropped all of the stolen beer.
The owner quickly called the police.
By now Pete knew this wouldn't end in peace.
He ran and ran and hid in the bushes.
He knew his shoves were no longer pushes.
Old Stealing Pete, They threw him in jail
Only able to get out on a $900 bail.

The Sun

By Madison Tart

(Refrain)

I love the sun in summer time.

I love it in the winter too.

Even in autumn it will shine,

And in spring causes flowers to bloom.

(Verse 1)

In the summer it shines down

And strikes hard upon the ground

It shines very, very bright

And be careful because burn you it might.

(Verse 2)

In the winter it might be cold

And a little foggy too.

The sun still shines very gold

On the way to reach you.

(Refrain)

(Verse 3)

In the autumn, though it does not shine for long,

It still keeps you nice and warm.

As the birds sing their song,

And, to them, there is no harm.

(Verse 4)

In the spring, it helps flowers to bloom

And dry up most rain.

It shines and lightens up your room,

And removes all the pain.

(Refrain)

Crash

By Gray Fussell

My mom was in college,
A freshman at UNC.
She was invited to fly over campus
And take pictures of all she could see.

She boarded the plane and was excited,
Oh, what a story she'd tell.
She'd take pictures of the Dean Dome,
Bell Tower, and Old Well.

The weather was picture perfect,
And after using up all of her film,
They were heading back to the airport
When suddenly the pilot looked grim.

"Angie, fasten your seat belt!"
The pilot suddenly cried.
"We're going to crash, I'm serious,
both of the engines have died!"

They fell from the sky and landed
Upside down among the trees.
But mom says, "It didn't hurt at all,"
"It was like God laid down feathers for me."

Earth

By Will Huff

Earth
Naturally beautiful
Amazing, growing, everlasting
Wild, unexplored, safe, comforting
Warming, loving, caring
Sentimental, Palace
Home

Sunrise, Sunset

By Madison Tart

Sunrise
pink, orange
shining, glowing, waking
rise, bright, set, dark
slowing, shimmering, falling
yellow, blue
Sunset

Landing

By Billy Prestage

My plane is finally
       l
        a
         n
          d
           i
            n
             g
              on the runway.

Home

By Will Huff

Home.
You keep me safe
From harm of the outdoor world.
You shelter me from the dangers of mother Earth.
You've developed me and
Matured me into who I am
Today. You have made
Memories with me and
My family. But you are
Only temporary. Better
Waits above in Heaven.

Flowers

By Marianne Moore

        Flowers
Beautiful   Bright
Blooming ....   Colorful
Orange   Yellow
        Pedals
        Short
        Green
        Stem
        Tall
        Long
        Roots
  Roses, Tulips, Daisies

Shaking Legs

By Harely Crumpler

S   a   i   g legs make you f   d
 h   k   n   a   o
                        l   w
                        l   n

Banana

By Amos Lanier

A
long and
slender yellow
fruit, so tasty in my
mouth. Taste great
on a split, with a big
red juicy cherry on
top. My mom uses it
to make bread, that is
so good. It is obvious
I am talking about the
banana. With their
thick peel, what
a tasty fruit!
Yum!

Crazy
By Pelmon Hudson

The
crazy
dog and cat
chase each other
around the block
and that is indeed no
lie. The cat meowed and the
dog barked. Then one day the man
had had enough. He put the pair in
a pin and knows they can argue no more.

Book
By Will Huff

Book,
You are
Like a brain.
Pages of text,
You enhance my mind.
You make me very smart.
Your pages release my thought.
Your spine my hands grip very tightly.
My imagination runs freely.
You have impressed my family and friends.

Goodbyes

By Blake Daniel

Lies
Are what
You tell me
And I believed.
Now I am moved on.
Do not come running back.
I will not be there to see
You wanting to be forgiven.
Begging and pleading will not help you.
Do not even save your goodbyes for me.

Love

By Madison Tart

    When in   love you
  use this symbol   to tell someone
how much you love them. To let that special
someone know that you care for them and
  love them with all your heart. It is one of
     the main things people see when
        they are talking about love.
          Hearts mean love
            forever and
              ever.

Caution

By Madison Tart

Words
are things
that are said
to tell someone
something important.
Some are good and some bad
but they will always be heard.
Gossip and lies are always feared
and mainly said by your friends themselves.
We need be careful about things we say.

Jesus

By Brooke Raynor

        Beginning
        and end He
        died for our
        sins. Cross
        of truth He
        rose again.
Yahweh Yisrael, Esh Oklah, Yahweh
Rophe, Savior, God our Father, God,
the good Shepherd, Jesus, Forgiver
of sins, Lord, Redeemer, El Shaddai.
        In His own
        time we will
        meet in a new
        Heaven kneeling
        at our Master's
        feet. What a very
        glorious day that
        will be with Jesus!

Winter Winds

By Will Huff

Winter winds so soft,
You float past me in a breeze.
The blossoms fly by.

Shower

By Amos Lanier

The big elephant
Squirting water with his trunk
Showering a mouse.

Wet

By Holden Quinn

Waves hitting the dock,
the ocean is such a blare,
amazingly wet.

Breeze

By Blake Daniel

Wind racing through hair
The breeze cooling hot athletes
Wishing it would stay.

Leaves

By Madison Tart

Many, many trees.
The leaves are simply falling
Down, down to the ground.

Rain

By Marianne Moore

Blue birds pecking trees
Rivers flowing with a breeze
Rain falling hardly

My First Car Crash

By Billy Prestage

Blood
on me
and people
screaming trying
to help me from my
terrible accident.
Blacking out but I'm about
to die. So they call for help then
I see a light and I start to crawl toward
it when all of the sudden I see blackness.

Winter

By Brooke Raynor

The chilly, cold wind
Shivers off the white cold snow
Oh! Winter is cold!

Bodie

By Gray Fussell

My dog is my friend.
He is playful and funny
And looks like a mop.

Goose

By Gray Fussell

There once was a student named Gray
Whose mom never thought he should play.
He'd cry and he'd shout,

"Why can't I go out?"
She said, "You must always make A's."

Where I'm From

By Billy Prestage

I am from the front pew of the Presbyterian church.
From Prestage Farms and hog slat.
I am from the wood that comes from the forest.
I am from the rose that fills my home with wonderful smells.
I am from Texas to eat the gigantic turkey that fills the table
And car rides to distant places.
From Scott & Joy Prestage.
I am from "Wake Up!!" and "Stop It."
From "It will be alright!" and "I'll always be there!"
I am from a Christian school.
I'm from Wilmington, hog, and turkey.
From the terrifying hurricane Katrina.
I am from falling through the rooftop.
I am from the cabinet.

Where I'm From
By Luke Burrows

I'm from cornfields,
From Dr. Pepper and backyard basketball.

I am from a happy home where stories and smiles are shared.
I am from the dogwood tree were branches lifted me to the sky.

I am from birthday ribs and laughter,
Ben, Suzanne and Dead Horse John.

I am from the procrastinators and overachievers.
From farmers and Presbyterians and Methodists where Sunday was not an option.

From Wally who washed up on the beach
And the Sutherlands in Scotland who lived in a castle.

From the happy times and the bad times
Where my family has always been there always loving me.

Where I'm From

By Sam Hall

I am from the center, the railroads, and dirt roads,
From the swamps, the pines, and dogwoods.
From the mossy elms to murky ponds,
I am from the corn in the woods to the ticks on weeds.

I am from the Irish and Choctaw, the strong and bold, from the Halls to the Thomases.
From the klutzes and smart alecs, from "Keep your eyes on the ball!" to "I love you."
I am from the tongues and believers, the knee sitters and jumpers.
From the rocky road, with the grapes and the Aztecs.

From the the three minors, the bikes that go through the tears.
I am from the cotton, feathered rice, the hood, the little white box
And the deep blue. From the red wild boar to the little blue heel.
I am from the grass and trees to the dust that makes me sneeze.

From Mars, Jupiter, Venus, and the sun always shining for another one.

Where I'm From

By Anna Burgess

I am from the lake, from the mossy bottom, and hot days.

I am from the freshly painted house where we sit in the air conditioning.

I am from the swamp tress behind the house, the bugs sifting through the branches.

I am from the Sunday afternoons and wake boarding in the rough water.

I am from the long rides to Cracker Barrel after being on the boat all day.

From being my dad's squirt and my Mom's little girl.

I am from the Roseboro Methodist Church.

I am from Clinton, North Carolina.

I'm from Italian food and steak houses.

From the ancestors who traveled here from Ireland, the family in Alabama and the family from Texas.

I am from all the family traits, all my childhood pictures,

And the same little ballerina I was when I was 2.

Atkinson

By Joseph Lee

The small town of Atkinson

The gentle breeze

The dark murk of Black River

The cool shade of the sprawling branches of a river birch

The fun of playing with my big, black dog

The peace of the wilderness

The marvel of God's creation

That's where I'm from.

Small Town

By Wilson Escalante

I am from a little small town where every day everybody is working
And every kid doesn't come out because it is too hot.
Just staying inside doing nothing but seeing the T.V. flicker.
All parents are at work.
I am inside playing games with all my friends and cousins.
Most of the time my friends and I give in and go outside even if it is too hot.
On the weekends I have to go to work with my dad.
Sometimes I go visit my cousin in Rose Hill.

Where I'm From

By Madison Guthrie

I am from the woods,
Where all the wild things are.
I am from the kitchen,
Warm, cozy, and tasteful.
I am from the roses
In my backyard.

I am from the Christmas tree,
Where it is lit so bright.
From Guy, to Christy, to Carol,
The stockings droop.

From young and foolish,
To independent and kind.
I am from the Christian side,
But I don't praise the Lord enough.

I'm from Kenansville,
Where we don't have much to do.
From the playground to the restaurants,
There is great people and great food.

I am from the pictures in every room,
Sitting there smiling, in my grandma's lap.
Feeling so comforted and loved
Having everybody as happy as me.

The Balloon

By Tyler Evans

                    n floated up to the sky.
              o
           o
        l
      l
    a
The b

Summer Day

By Tyler Evans

The wind blows all day.
The trees never stop swaying.
The grass is so green.
All the flowers are blooming.
The sun is shining so bright.

Animals

By Tyler Evans

Rabbits
Hopping around
The grass
Discovering places.

Turtles
Slowly reaching a spot
To live.

God

By Harley Crumpler

God.
El Chay.
El-Shaddai.
Almighty Lord.
Jehovah-Rapha.
Christ, Son of Living God.
Everlasting Father.
The Way, the Truth, and the Life.
The Resurrection and the Life.
Author and Finisher of Our Faith.
We can always count on Him with our lives!

Fluffer

By Harley Crumpler

There once was a puppy named Fluffer.
Who always loved to be the tougher.
Once she peed on the floor,
Then got kicked out the door.
If she pees inside, she will suffer.

Brothers

By Harley Crumpler

There was a cat
That said, "I'm faster than a rat!"
Then came up a dog
That said, "Well, I can catch a hog!"
Walking by were a possum and a squirrel.
When they heard them, they went to God in a whirl.
They said His creations were fighting about which one is faster.
Then God walked to the scene and everything was a disaster.
He said, "Why do you fight with one another?
Can you not see I created all of you to be brothers?"
The animals surely did fall in shame.
For they only had themselves to blame.
They all became friends.
And by God they were cleansed.
They worked together the rest of their lives.
And the kinship they formed that day still survives.

Replaced

By Will Huff

The roads were icy,
And the tires wouldn't lace,
So here I am now
Saying I should've gotten them replaced.

Old Man Tan

By Will Huff

There was once a very old man,
Who always tried to get a nice tan.
But he burnt his old face
And broke his ankle brace
And needed a retirement plan.

The Devil Himself
By Will Huff

If you've ever been tempted to do wrong,
Then you have been following quickly along,
With the hurtful ways of the beast.
Hopefully you can say the least.

He has done so much wrong to us all,
Killed, stolen and made us crawl.
Turning good times into times of misery,
Turning good lives into things lost in history.

Maybe you have not met him yet,
Or maybe you two form a duet.
Hopefully you're not on his shelf,
Meeting with the Devil himself.

A Change
By Will Huff

What has happened with yourself?
It's like you been thrown over the continental shelf.
You have no mercy, you're so mean to me.
I beg for mercy. Mercy I plea!
You've turned so sour
And bitter all around.
You used to be like a flower,
A beautiful gold crown!
But now you are changing,
From better to worse,
The problems are raging,
And I'm wondering if it's a curse!
You are being so resistant,
And I'm afraid our love is growing distant.

The Snake and the Boy

By Will Huff

A little boy found a small snake,
Gave it food, fixed its ache.
The boy knew it could kill him,
But he still cared, poor old Tim!
He kept on with his duties,
And the snake, well, it bit him.

Beach

By Will Huff

You are my palace.
You are my sanctuary.
You unwind my life.
Sand blows across the surface,
You shape the borders of me.

The Spider and the Fly

By Will Huff

The spider
Staring closely
At his foe.

Small fly is
Flying aimlessly
Around
Silk string.

Bullet

By Pelmon Hudson

People die for reasons many,
But not many die with a bullet to the fanny.

Football

By Pelmon Hudson

Football is fun.
Although we have to run.
Each day we must face the sun.
And although I might get spun,
The hits I'll never shun.
Man, that linebacker must weigh a ton.
Busting my lip sure is no fun.
But I know the game will be won.
Then we will be number one!
And dad will say, "Proud of you, Son!"

Sports

By Gray Fussell

I
Love sports.
Competing
Is exciting.
And winning is the
Best feeling to me. I
Feel proud, strong, and satisfied
When I've worked hard to accomplish
A goal. Playing sports also gives me
Confidence, like I can do anything.

I Love the Beach

By Gray Fussell

I'm a kid who's named Gray
At night I always pray.
I tell God about my day
And try to live the right way.
My favorite place is Magan's Bay;
I want to go back there and stay.
All day I could play
And on the beach I could lay
Till the sun went away
And I'd do it again the next day.

Muscadine

By Gray Fussell

My dad's job is making wine.
To make it, he uses the muscadine.
These delicious, fat, and juicy grapes
Make the wines fruity and gives it a sweet taste.

There is Carolina Red and Beaufort Bay,
Midnight Magnolia, and Serenade
I work there some, but not a lot
Because mainly what I do is plot.

Many people love the way they taste
Right now his wines are sold in 12 different states
And that list is growing, this is clear
Because Duplin Wines will be sold in China next year.

Washey Will

By Gray Fussell

Wishey washy Will
went wildly in the
woods where he
whittled wooden
whistles

Swish!

By Gray Fussell

Time
Is running out.
Dribbling
towards the goal,

I shoot,
and hear
the swish!

Juicy Worm

By Amos Lanier

Down in the meadow,
Underneath the maple tree,
Sits a red robin who is
Looking for a juicy worm.
Surely spring is almost here.

Trains

By Amos Lanier

Trains
Are cool.
I like them.
Do you like trains?
They go very fast.
They drive on long train tracks.
Sometimes people ride in trains.
They have many big cars on them.
Trains carry big things like coal and rocks.
The tall, lean conductor is in charge of the train.

Deer

By Amos Lanier

The deer
is a thing
of beauty,

But a
scare
to drivers
at night.

My Love

By Amos Lanier

My love has gone across the sea
To return to her place of birth
To live there with her family.
I feel she has fallen from earth.

Will this love survive the test?
Will her heart stay ever true?
Of all the girls, she's been the best.
At loving me through and through!

She promised that she would call.
I'll wait ever so patiently.
Hoping that her word would not fall.
I'll still love only her faithfully.

She did call, and I'm filled with glee.
She has decided to come home to me!

Poor Old Ray

By Holden Quinn

The children laugh and play.
The parents always sound so gay.
No one ever asks what happened
To my cousin, poor old Ray.

Rhyming

By Holden Quinn

There once was a boy from HCA.
He wasted his time throughout the day.
Mr. Hunter arrives,
And he asks us to thrive.
So now we are rhyming away.

Solo Flight

By Holden Quinn

Up in the sky
I fly in my plane.
The clouds are so high.
It begins to rain.

In the clouds I soar.
Not a care in the world,
Who could ask for more?
All of my toes curl,

As the instruments I watch
To keep everything right
One more flight in my belt I notch
'til alas' I make my first solo flight.

Bear and Lion

By Holden Quinn

There once was a bear and a lion.
Neither wanted to share.
Until one day the lion needed food.
The bear would not give up.
The lion ate the bear
Since he wouldn't share.
Now there is no more bear,
Since the bear couldn't share.

Drip

By Blake Daniel

>   Drip
>
>   Drip fall-
>
>   ing from the
>
>   dark unwanted
>
>   skies bringing gloom
>
>   to most but peace to
>
>   some...falling and falling
>
>   until they touch the
>
>   ground.

Field

By Blake Daniel

On the field here I play.
Hoping this is where I stay.
Up and down the field I run,
Always having lots of fun.

Fighting for the ball,
Hoping the other girl will fall.
Seeing her on the ground,
Joy is what I found.

Scoring a goal hoping to win,
The final score was one to ten.
Victory is defiantly sweet
The next team is who we meet.

Friends

By Madison Tart

The people who are there for you
When you are down and feeling blue
They pick you up and never let you down.
The people who won't let you frown

They are by your side
And will not let you collide,
With bad things in life
That will bring you struggle and strife.

They will even walk a mile
Just to try to get you to smile.
Some are best and some are not
But they will be there for you no matter what!

Apology

By Madison Tart

As I made my way
Through the dreary day
I thought of all the things I could say.
My mind was fray
And the thought kept coming and it would decay
That my apology might not be okay.
And though it was the perfect time of day
The perfect words I could not say.
If I might, if I may
Those words I would go back and say.

Gorilla and the Monkey

By Madison Tart

Gorilla thought he was better than monkey.
He tried to swing from tree to tree.
He would always fall flat
Because he was so fat.
At swinging, monkey was better than he.

Caterpillar

By Madison Tart

Caterpillar is
young and growing
to become
beautiful.

Butterfly is
flying and soaring
with brilliant colors.

Heartbreak

By Madison Tart

As the moonlight shone,
In my eyes you could see the tears.
I have never known
What it felt like to be loved for years.

You told me you were tired
Of the same old things.
Turns out you had just wired
My heart with many strings.

I was over the way you treated me.
I felt like it was not smart,
That you said we should not be
And broke my hopeful heart.

I know now my heart is broken in two,
But I know it was best for me and you.

Late

By Marianne Moore

I realized I was late
For going out on my date.
I hoped that he didn't hate
That I had become overweight.
As soon as I saw my mate
We both looked very straight.
All I did was wait,
Wishing I would deflate.
Oh now what's going to happen is just great…
Because all we're going to do is have a great debate.

Grave

By Marianne Moore

There once was man from the deep sea
Who fished and fished all day until three.
He fell off his big dock
And got hit by a rock.
In his grave forever he will be.

Septuplet

By Marianne Moore

Dog
Barking Loudly
Roaming freely
Across the yard.

Cat
Eating its food
Meowing contently.

Brothers

By Brooke Raynor

In the time of need
I do not have to concede.
They like to have fun
After the job is done.

It is starting to rain
But I have no pain.
I am willing to succeed
But for right now I will do a good deed.

Watch a football game
But he will aim
One day to be on the field
Hoping to get his dream sealed.

What I would not do
For someone like you.
I need to tell mother
How thankful I am to have you as a brother.

America

By Brooke Raynor

The sounds of gun shots ring in the air day and night.
Smoke fills the air with the smell of gun powder,
With the sounds of soldiers screaming at their might.
The Americans could not have been prouder.
Women were smart and also took a part.
Many injured soldiers were cared for by a nurse.
Women sewed needed items that left their mark.
We praised God that the war was not any worse.
We were trying to gain independence.
Water was the battle ground for the last fight.
There was silence among the attendance.
When the smoke cleared the flag stood with all her might.

The national anthem was born this day.
Which led Americans to live in a new way.

Whale

By Brooke Raynor

Whale
strong and majestic
swimming with ease.

Fish
hurriedly hiding
while searching
for food.

Penny

By Luke Burrows

Pennies are so shiny
Enjoying them is easy to do
Not as big as a quarter
Nor a nickel
Yet still the best coin

Star

By Luke Burrows

          A
        Star
      in the sky
It's beauty is so breathtaking
   In Space so far away
  So bright and so yellow
 it is so big and powerful
 it shines   along with
  the   moon.

The Silky Sky
By Joseph Lee

A silent night sky
Surrounds silver beams of light.
Moonlight engulfs all
Sending peace and beauty down
To the dreamy earth asleep.

A Winter's Maiden
By Joseph Lee

Are you as beautiful as a brisk winter's morning?
With your white hair cascading down your shoulders,
The snow sparkles on your skin while the sun is scalding
The snow covered mountain boulders.

You must be much more splendid and beautiful
For your eyes make the sky jealous
And the snowflakes say your beauty is irrefutable
The snowy world proclaims your elegance endless.

Your scarlet lips make the winter roses envy
The camellia looks on in wonder
As you stand by the snow laden ivy
And you hair gives off a glorious luster.

Your beauty shadows the glory of a winter day
And your divine loveliness eclipses winter's bouquet.

Songbird

By Joseph Lee

Singing joyful songs

Over the land flow your melodies

Never uttering a mournful sound

Going wherever you please

Beloved by old and young

Ill attitudes are cast away

Rejoicing over everything

Delighted by most lived by all

Flower

By Madison Guthrie

The flower
Bloomed
On That
Very day

Sprouting from
The ground
Like Earth growing.

Chocolate

By Anna Carson Quinn

Boom!
A chocolate bomb came crashing down.
It was like bathing in rays from Heaven.
Chocolate is the greatest ever!

Chocolate

By Sam Hall

Chocolate is like Heaven on earth,
With its smooth, silky, brown cover,
That conceals it from the rest of the world.

So many types exist.
How could you choose just one?
So many colors, smells, and tastes.

It's like all of the diversity in the world.
So many.
So much.

Sweet Temptations

By Luke Burrows

Chocolate is a sweet treat.
It stares at me,
Begging me to eat it.
I have to be as strong as a lion
To resist its temptation.

Oh! But I just couldn't stop myself.
Its temptation is too strong.
It draws me like a fisherman
Reeling in a fish.
Yum!

Crunchy, Chewy Chocolate

By Anna Burgess

Crunchy. Chewy. Chocolate.
Hershey's is like Heaven.
Only chocolate can make me feel better.
On rainy days when I'm sick,
Lovely sweet chocolate is always,
Always there for me.
Tasty. Amazing. Chocolate.

Spring

By Hannah Buckner

The sun is shining so bright and warm.
The sky is blue with no clouds in sight.
The grass is soft like a bed of clouds.
Flowers are growing so colorful and bright.
Small, baby animals are running freely
While their mothers watch closely.
Bumblebees come out to collect more honey,
And caterpillars turn to butterflies
And flutter around freely.
Baby chicks chirp around the farm.
That is what spring is all about-
Waiting for summer to come again.

www.ingramcontent.com/pod-product-compliance
Lightning Source LLC
Chambersburg PA
CBHW041620220426
43661CB00046B/1514